Devil Monkey

BY
GEORGE DUDDING

PUBLISHED BY GSD PUBLICATIONS

Spencer, West Virginia

January 19, 2017

www.gdparanormal.com

In Memory of
PAMELA J. DUDDING

No. 2017-001

Introduction by the Author

For several weeks, I had been asking around if anyone knew of a strange creature, something that I haven't already written about, that I could use for my next book topic. Since I had just completed my thirty-eighth book titled *Bigfoot 5: The West Virginia Yeti,* I was running out topics. I didn't think that something like that was possible since these weird animals seem to keep crawling out of the woodwork. Someone suggested that the *Devil Monkey* should be the topic of my next literary accomplishment. The thought of an animal out there that jumps around like a kangaroo, has a face like a vicious dog, and resembles a baboon was too much to resist. I soon learned that this creature may have been around much longer than I had thought—possibly over a century.

In several of my past books, I have been able to find a connection between several weird creatures and my hometown of Point Pleasant, West Virginia. In addition to Mothman, I have found that the area may have also played host to Bigfoot, Sheepsquatch, Dogman, and maybe Goatman. Could the Devil Monkey have been among them? To determine the answer, I dug through some of my old research material and interviewed a fellow high school classmate who had lived in the area where a strange sighting is suppose to have taken place at Point Pleasant back in 1966. That just happened to be around the same time in which the legendary Mothman made his debut at the TNT Area. Finally, I made another quick trip to Point Pleasant and explored that area of interest located off Route 62 at the northern end of town. The results of my findings have revealed that the Devil Monkey, or something like it, may have visited that area 50 years ago. There seems to be no limit to the high strangeness that exists around that old Ohio River town.

Speaking of Point Pleasant, I have just recently returned from another jaunt into that mysterious area. Early in January of 2017, I was back there to participate in an interview, which is expected to appear in a new documentary movie *The Mothman of Point Pleasant* that is set to come out later this year.

I have searched through many archives in my effort to obtain a good representation of Devil Monkey sightings that have occurred within the United States, along with a few in other countries, and I have included them here in this book.

At this time, I invite you to read this latest book titled *Devil Monkey*. I hope you enjoy it.

Devil Monkey

"A thin body, low squatty legs, and a long black tail were all that he could distinguish, but it was altogether unlike any animal he ever saw before."

- Creature description - *Ironton Register* - 1875

To explain the origin of the *Devil Monkey* is very difficult because the theories behind the creature widely vary. The term was originally introduced by the author, theorist, and cryptozoologist Mark A. Hall. The Devil Monkey is generally described as having shaggy fur, clawed feet with three toes, a face and nose like that of a canine, small pointed ears, the body of a baboon, a long, bushy tail, and it is around three to four feet tall with some claims that it can be as tall as eight feet. One of its special talents is the ability to leap distances of 20 feet in a single bound.

Some believe that the Devil Monkey is a primate species that has just recently been discovered and therefore it has not officially been classified or documented at this point. It could also be a cryptid whose existence has yet to be proven. There are those that believe it is a species left over from a group of prehistoric primates that no longer exist. Still others are sure that it does not belong to the animal kingdom or even to the group of animals that are studied by cryptozoologists. Instead, they believe that it belongs in the group of mythological animals. There are also those who believe that the creature is otherworldly.

Some proponents of the of mythological origins of the Devil Monkey say that it comes to us as a legend that originated from the Choctaws, a tribe of very civilized Native Americans that lived in the southeastern part of the United States. The Choctaws believed that there was a creature known as the *Nalusa Falaya*. The Nalusa Falaya was a thin, black creature with pointed ears, beady eyes, and a long tail. It moved about by using a type of locomotion that is similar to that of a snake by searching out and pursuing its victims by slinking along the surface of the ground on its stomach. One difference between the two entities is the fact that its crawling method of travel does not jive with the jumping and hopping form of locomotion employed by the Devil Monkey. Also, the Devil Monkey does not have the supernatural powers that the Choctaws attributed to the Nalusa Falaya.

There is one faction who believes that the Devil Monkey may be from one of many parallel universes or a multiverse, and that they arrive here through a portal in much the same way some theorists have tried to explain the existence of Bigfoot. Along that same line, there are those who have a theory that the entity is an alien that arrives here from another world by way of an UFO. In many cases, investigators have been able to associate its presence with the appearance of one or more UFOs in the same area and the same time frame.

Just as in some of the more far-out, unbelievable theories behind the Goatman or the Melonheads, there are those who believe that the Devil Monkey is a creature that escaped from a government research area or that it was a mutation which was caused by heavy metal or other chemical pollution in some particular geographical area.

Since 1934, there have been outbreaks in the appearance of what witnesses have claimed to be kangaroos that have occurred all over the United

States, especially in the Midwest. These appearances of kangaroos where they should not be, especially when they are not native to the area have been referred to as *phantom kangaroo* sightings. It is believed that there have been creatures that were incorrectly reported as Devil Monkeys when in actuality they were kangaroos. The same theory can also go both ways because some creatures may have been incorrectly reported as kangaroos when in actuality they were Devil Monkeys.

Similarly, some believe that the Devil Monkey sightings may have simply been sightings of actual monkeys or baboons. In the United States and other countries where there are no native species of these primates, their presence is explained by suggesting that they are escapees from a circus, zoo, or individuals who kept them as pets. The same explanation is used for the presence of actual kangaroos. Some of these so called kangaroos may have been mistaken for a relative of the kangaroo known as the wallaby.

Another explanation for Devil Monkey encounters is the possibility that it may be a misidentification of a different cryptid. In some Devil Monkey sightings, the creature description was similar to that of a *Dogman*, a *Werewolf*, a *Loup Garou*, or even a *Chupacabra*.

4

The following stories represent some of the most well known encounters with the Devil Monkey on record today.

PATTERSON RIVER, ALASKA

Thomas Bay is found in Southeast Alaska just north of Petersburg and it branches off of Frederick Bay toward the east. Thomas Bay was named after a U. S. naval officer, Charles M. Thomas. Its coordinates are 57°01'53"N, 132°51'13"W. The Baird Glacier drains into Thomas Bay. The Patterson River and the Muddy River also drain into Thomas Bay on its southern end. A native tribe known as the *Tlingit* has inhabited the area for hundreds of years. In 1750, a large mountainside began to slip and buried a village of around 500 of these natives. As a result, Thomas Bay became known to the Tlingit as *Geey Nana*, which translates to Bay of Death. That name alone should serve as a foreboding reminder that one might be better off to stay way.

The natives of that region had something to hide and that was the fact that there was gold back in the hills and valleys. These natives weren't obsessed with gold, but the white man showed up around 1900 and they were intent on searching for it. Acting on a hot tip, these prospectors entered the Thomas Bay and travelled up the Patterson River in search of their fortune. What they found was something else. The few that survived the expedition into the Alaskan wilderness told a strange tale. Many of these survivors had been thoroughly frightened to the point that they had suffered mental breakdowns. Somewhere near two bodies of water, one of which was Ess Lake and another shaped like a half-moon, they came under attack by some sort of devil creatures that lived in the wilderness. The creatures were described as not being a man or a monkey, but something with characteristics of the two. Their tracks appeared to be half-way between a bear and a human. These devil creatures stood around four feet tall, had forelegs and hind legs that terminated in claws, and were covered with a rough, shaggy hair. It is also said that the creatures were foul smelling, which some accounts attributed to sores on the monster's body. The creatures also seemed to utilize teamwork in their attacks. One other thing that the prospectors had noticed was that there did not seem to be any small game living in that particular area of the wilderness— perhaps there was a reason.

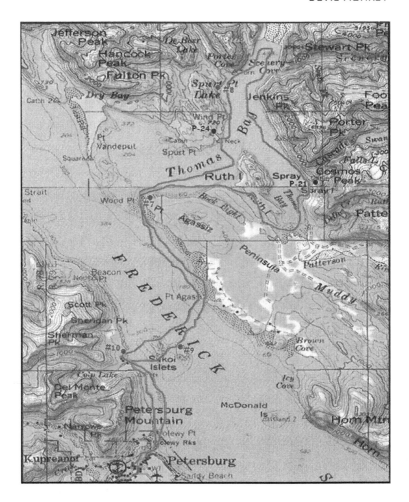

MAP OF ALASKA SHOWING THOMAS BAY, THE
PATTERSON RIVER, AND THE MUDDY RIVER
PUBLIC DOMAIN FROM WIKIPEDIA

Other encounters with these strange creatures
were also reported. A fur trapper working in the
same general area along the Muddy River had a
strange experience that may have resulted in his

final demise. He was working his traps during a snowstorm when his dog erupted into a barking spell and appeared to be chasing something. The trapper began to follow the dog's tracks which eventually came to an abrupt end as though it had been captured by a large animal. That creature's tracks took over where the dog's tracks left off. They were a large, seven-inch track that resembled both a small bear and a human. The tracking configuration indicated that the creature alternated between walking on four legs and walking upright on its hind legs. The man began to track the monster until he realized something more serious and that was when he learned that the creature had started stalking him. He made a getaway and escaped back to civilization where he told his story. Later, the trapper returned to the woods to continue checking his traps. The trapper was never heard of again and it is believed that the creature or creatures caught up with him.

A Tlingit boogeyman known as the *Kushtaka* (or Kooshdakhaa) has been blamed for some of these encounters. Local legends say that the Kushtaka, a mythical shape-shifting creature, inhabits the temperate rainforest part of Southeastern Alaska. A more plausible explanation for these creatures is that they are actually Alaskan versions of the Devil Monkey. As a result of the encounters with these creatures in that geographical region of Alaska, the area has become known as Devil's Country or Devil's Thumb as it appears on some maps.

COPPER RIVER, ALASKA

The Copper River or Ahtna River watershed begins in the Chugach Mountains and the Copper Glacier in the Wrangell Mountains. It flows 290 miles until it reaches the Gulf of Alaska in the south central part of Alaska. The coordinates of the riverhead are 62°10'39"N, 143°49'05"W. The river received its name from the abundant copper deposits located there which were often used by Alaskan natives to fashion various tools. The *Ahtna* people are a native Alaskan tribe of hunters and fishermen that live along the Copper River. During the early history of Alaska, before the territory was purchased by the United States in 1869, the Russians tried to invade the Copper River area, but were not successful because the Ahtna tribes fought them off. After the United States purchased the territory, the white explorers gradually drifted into the areas around the Copper River in the 1880s. The Ahtna people are culturally similar to the Tlingit people who live farther south. Today, their total population is around 500.

CAMPING ALONG THE COPPER RIVER EARLY 1900s
PUBLIC DOMAIN PHOTO FROM WIKIPEDIA

According to legend, the Ahtna people believe that there is a dangerous creature living out in the Alaskan wilderness. These creatures are the "monkey people" or the *Cet'aeni* (alternate spellings are Cet'aenn or Tcetin and it is pronounced ket-ann-ee). The name means "tailed ones" and refers to a legendary humanoid that lives in the trees and the underground caves of the wilderness along the Copper River. They were discussed by Nick Redfern and Ken

Gerhard during a recent episode of *Lost in Alaska*. These scary creatures have a simpler name—they are the Alaskan Devil Monkey.

FLAGSTAFF, ARIZONA

A woman claims that she was accompanied by her dog as she was hiking along the Mount Eldon forest trail near Flagstaff, Arizona. She noticed that her dog was behaving in an agitated manner as they were approaching a rocky area. She soon figured out what was aggravating the dog when she saw a small group of primate-like animals playing among the rocks. The witness reported that the ape-like animals were about four to five feet tall and they were fast on their feet as they hopped and scurried around the rocks. Creatures of that description had been seen around Flagstaff previously and had been lumped into the category of the Devil Monkey.

NEWNAN, GEORGIA

Farther south, in Coweta County, Georgia, another series of strange encounters with a monkey-like creature occurred during August of

1979 in the town of Newnan. It was mostly seen in the areas around Belk Road and several of its initial sightings were near the intersection of Belk Road and West Washington Street. Mary Strozier and her family were among the first witnesses to see the creature. It was described as having a face like a monkey in some cases, while some said its face resembled that of a dog. It had a long, bushy tail much like that of a beaver, was covered in black fur, and stood around five feet tall. Its eyes were reported to sparkle or glow brightly at night. Most witness accounts described the large monkey-like creature as being bipedal, but some claimed that at times it was both bipedal and quadrupedal. The creature, which some thought bore the likeness of a large wild dog, was actually reported by one witness who saw it digging holes in one her flower beds. Soon, the monster laid claim to its very own name and was labeled the *Belk Road Booger*. Law enforcement officers from the Coweta County Sheriff department, the Newnan Police Department, and the Georgia Department of Natural Resources investigated several of the incidents and they could not substantiate the existence of the creature. A local DNR officer placed traps at key locations in an effort to capture the monster. Some of the locals believed that the monster was making its home in nearby barns or the junk cars in a nearby salvage yard. It was thought to be feeding on a nearby abundant supply of apples and corn.

Additional sightings of the *Belk Road Booger* occurred less than three miles to the northwest of Newnan in the Meadowview Subdivision near the Arnco Mills area. The witness in that sighting, Nancy Jackson, was scared half out of her wits by what she described as one of the ugliest animals that she had ever seen. Other sightings that occurred within the same locality were on Smokey Road, Welcome Sargent Road, and Ishman Ballard Road. Around that same time, a creature of the same description was seen running away from a barn in the eastern part of Newnan. It was seen again, jumping over a wall, in that same area in the early part of the 1980s. Another woman also saw the creature along a street in the same area. A newspaper story about the mysterious animal, titled *Strange Creature Seen Here* first appeared in the August 9, 1979 edition of *The Newnan Times-Herald*. Other articles on the creature soon followed in the same newspaper until the monster finally quit showing up.

It wasn't until 2005 that it was believed that the Belk Road Booger had returned. Around that time, a woman was driving eastward on State Route 16 from Newnan, Georgia toward Senoia,

Georgia. About six miles from Newnan, near the Poplar Road intersection, she saw a creature that met the description of the Devil Monkey. One exception was the fact that it was eight feet tall. As she drove up a hill, the creature passed from the left side of the road to the center of the road which prompted her to slow down. As she drove past the creature, it was so close to the driver side of the car that it was almost a near collision.

More sightings of a similar nature occurred, but since the new monster was a much larger creature, it was given a different name. It became known as the *Happy Valley Horror* because it was first seen walking in a field, five miles north of Newnan, in a wooded, upscale, rural residential area known as Happy Valley Circle. Later, it was observed multiple times, by different members of the Robards family, as it walked along Cedar Creek Road near its intersection with Happy Valley Circle. As it turns out, the Happy Valley Horror is thought to have been a Bigfoot, whereas the Belk Road Booger has been classified as a Devil Monkey. However, some descriptions of the Devil Monkey allow its height range to be three to eight feet tall.

It is interesting how certain people come forward with strange claims and try to discredit the original witnesses in these types of sightings.

For instance, the *Flatwoods Monster* sighting at Flatwoods, West Virginia in 1952 has been made out to have been just an owl setting on a tree branch. Then the *Mothman* sighting in 1966 at Point Pleasant, West Virginia was also chalked up to another owl that had taken up residence inside an old abandoned power plant. Just recently, I personally had the experience of listening to someone trying to discredit the Mothman incident. A man setting next to me at a recent high school alumni dinner in Point Pleasant was talking to everyone at the table and told them the following story. *There wasn't any Mothman up there in that TNT that night. That was just me playing jokes on a bunch of them kids that was parking up there. I went around until I found some couples parked in a car and then I jumped up and down on their bumper. It scared them real good and they ran downtown and told the police that Mothman story.*

How does all of this apply here? Well, around thirty years after the Belk Road Booger sightings, some locals told a story about a boy that dressed up in a gorilla suit and ran around scaring people. Then, after the novelty of being the Belk Road Booger wore off, he allegedly went to Bishopville, South Carolina and perpetrated another monster hoax by posing as the *Lizard Man of Scape Ore Swamp*. I would say that these

15

claims, like those in the previous paragraph, are most likely a hoax which someone has concocted.

MOUNT VERNON, ILLINOIS

In October of 1941, a hunter in Jefferson County, Illinois near the City of Mount Vernon had a close encounter with a baboon-like creature in the woods. There seems to be some confusion in the recorded accounts of the incident as to which of two brothers was the witness. I could not determine if it was Reverend Lepton Harpole or Reverend Marsh Harpole. For simplicity, I will just refer to the witness as Reverend Harpole. Harpole was squirrel hunting in the woods along the bottoms around Gum Creek when a creature that resembled a baboon jumped out of a tree striking him squarely in the head. The Reverend's hat was knocked clean off of his head and a pipe that he was smoking flew out of his mouth. The creature, which had dark brown hair, was making weird sounds as it jumped up and down. The fun and games were all over when the unpredictable creature decided to deliver an attack on the man of the cloth. The Reverend Harpole wasn't someone to underestimate, because he swiftly smacked the creature with the

16

barrel of his trusty shotgun. The monster leaped backward and then took off in the opposite direction. The reverend instinctively raised his shotgun, squeezed the trigger, and fired a thunderous warning shot into the air. The loud reverberation of the shot sent the monster retreating into the bushes.

For the duration of a year afterwards, a number of people around Mount Vernon continued to report a creature that was believed to be the same one. They said it was baboon-like in appearance and it could leap distances of 20 feet. At night, the locals could hear the monster screaming in the wooded bottom land lying along Gum Creek. After that, the monster was spotted in other nearby communities. One individual encountered the beast as it ran across the road in front of his vehicle along the Big Muddy River in Jackson County 40 miles southwest of Mount Vernon. It was reported to have killed a dog about seven miles south of Mount Vernon at the small town of Bonnie, Illinois. Armed search parties, carrying all types of paraphernalia to capture or kill the monster, were sent out to search for the animal and they scoured the trees and brush along the Gum Creek bottoms without success. Hunters claimed that they had difficulty tracking the beast because it was constantly on the move and it could leap distances of 20 feet or more in a single bound. After that, the monster was not heard of again. The Reverend Harpole's brother, the other Reverend Harpole, served as his character reference and vouched for his credibility. The incident is now considered to be an early Devil Monkey encounter.

ENFIELD, ILLINOIS

It was about 32 years after the Mount Vernon, Illinois encounters that another hideous, scary creature showed itself at Enfield, Illinois. Enfield is in White County and it happens to be located about 35 miles to the southeast of Mount Vernon.

On the evening of April 25, 1973, at around 8:30 PM, a ten year old boy by the name of Greg Garrett was playing outdoors in his backyard while his parents were inside watching television. Suddenly, out of nowhere came a nasty creature with clawed feet and it attacked the boy. Luckily the boy was able to get away and run to the safety of his house, but not before the strange creature's claws had ripped up his tennis shoes. His parents later reported the strange encounter, but not until things with the weird creature had escalated.

Around 30 minutes later, the same creature made an appearance outside the nearby McDaniel residence where two children had been left home alone. It was about 9:30 PM when Henry McDaniel and his wife returned to their home and found their two children scared half to death. The youngsters, Henry and Lil McDaniel, were very shaken up as they told their parents that something had tried to break into the house through the door and when that didn't succeed, it tried to get in through a window where an air conditioner was installed. The parents may not have taken them seriously, but moments later the parents began to become devout believers when something began clawing at the front door.

The father, Henry McDaniel, was a little annoyed by that time and he jerked open the door. Much to his surprise, the creepy creature was right there on the front steps staring right back at him. Acting pretty much on reflex action, he slammed the door shut in the monster's face. He ran to the bedroom and grabbed a .22 caliber hand gun along with a flashlight. He ran back to the front door and slung it open and was once again face-to-face with the ugly red-eyed entity. The animal, or whatever it was, stood about 4.5 feet tall, had what appeared to be three feet with sharp claws, had two short arms, and was gray in color. The thing made a move to enter the house and Henry McDaniel fired one round and hit it directly. It came back at him with a sharp hissing sound and the frightened homeowner fired four more rounds at it. The thing did not fall, but it did turn and run away from his house as it covered around 50 feet in about three leaps. It then disappeared into the darkness along the Louisville & Nashville Railroad tracks that ran in front of his house. He promptly called law enforcement and several state troopers arrived at his house to investigate. They only found some scratches on the siding of his house and some three-toed tracks in the front yard. The witnesses reported something strange about the creature. They believed that the creature had three legs, which is the most mystifying thing about it. That wasn't the last sighting for Mr. McDaniel.

Only eleven days later on May 6, 1973, Mr. McDaniel was awakened in the night to the sound of barking dogs. He got out of bed, grabbed his hand gun and went to the front door to take a look outside. In the distance, illuminated by a nearby street light, he could clearly see the same creature as it walked along the Louisville & Nashville Railroad tracks in front of his house. He did not fire a single shot and the creature slowly travelled on down the tracks until it was out of sight.

This third sighting brought a barrage of news media to the area, not to mention monster enthusiasts who were on the hunt for the mysterious entity. At one point, the local sheriff threatened to jail Mr. McDaniel for spreading tales and terrifying everyone. Two monster hunters, Mike Mogle and Roger Tappy arrived from the adjoining state of Indiana to try their luck searching for the creature. They hit pay dirt when they spotted a gray monkey-like creature just before it made its getaway into some thick brush. They were unable to get off a shot.

On May 8, 1973, a group of five hunters searched the area near and along the railroad tracks where the initial sightings had occurred. Finally, they had a visual sighting and they reported that the monster was covered in hair or fur. Previously, it was thought that the monster displayed only its bare skin. These hunters fired bullets at the creature and claimed that they had no effect. This prompted the arrival of a deputy sheriff who arrested all five hunters for illegal hunting and being a threat to public safety.

Another person who was witness to the same monster was a news director of WWKI radio, out of Kokomo, Indiana. He was accompanied by three other subjects who came to the area in search of the elusive monster. His efforts paid off when he and his cohorts spotted a gray figure, about five-foot tall, moving around near an empty house in the same neighborhood of the initial encounters. The posture of the animal as it stood up was baboon-like. During their search efforts, they were able to get a tape recording of the beast's horrifying scream.

Witnesses in the sightings reported that the monster seemed to have three legs. Law enforcement found three-toed tracks in the yard in a configuration that indeed indicated that the creature might have had three legs. One of the three footprints was smaller than the others. My theory is that the third leg was not a leg, but instead was the paw of one arm that the hunched-forward monkey-like creature placed on the ground for balance and support. There is another theory that the three-toed monster may have been misinterpreted as being a three-legged monster.

Notable cryptozoological investigators such as Loren Coleman and John Keel studied the details of the incident and wrote articles about it. The creature was thought to be possibly baboon-like or maybe even kangaroo-like. Some believed that it might have been the result of a genetic experiment that escaped from a government research facility. Others thought that it might be an alien visitor from outer space. The bizarre encounter that unfolded over that period of time back in 1973 became known as the *Enfield Horror*. Some believe that the creature was a Devil Monkey and place it in a list of encounters of that type. I have noticed that the scene of the Enfield sighting strangely resembles the railroad track area along Madison Avenue in Point Pleasant, West Virginia, where I recently investigated a Dogman sighting that is detailed in my recent book *Dogman: Michigan, Wisconsin, and West Virginia*.

CHICAGO, ILLINOIS

On January 12, 2006, a bizarre encounter with a creature that was described as a combination of monkey, wolf, and devil took place at Chicago, Illinois. The report came from an anonymous witness and it was eventually reported in several publications as a Devil Monkey sighting. According to the story, the witness and his family arrived at their Chicago home one evening and upon entering through the front door, they found a vicious entity with long, sharp fangs attacking their pet Labrador Retriever. The creature had a monkey-like tail and bright, glowing eyes. Unlike other encounters between monsters and their witnesses where no one has a camera, the man was able to grab a nearby camera and take a photograph of the critter. When the camera flash went off, the startled creature stopped his attack on the pet dog, turned toward the witness, and leaped through the air toward him. It then made a quick exit through the front door of the house as it practically knocked everyone down on its way out.

The witness has also made additional claims that residents of his neighborhood have complained about missing pets and one of them even reported that they saw a monster meeting the same description that was hanging by it tail from the branch of a neighborhood tree. Some cryptid investigators believe that there is something wrong with this entire story and it has been deemed to be a hoax. The photograph taken of the creature appears to be one of a dog rather than that of a devil monkey. I agree that the photograph looks very suspicious. In spite of all this, there are some cryptid investigators who believe that this is a legitimate encounter. Therefore, it has made its way into the list of Devil Monkey encounters.

CHICAGO, ILLINOIS

Many sightings that have been reported as either monkeys or kangaroos have, at a later date, been determined to be possible Devil Monkey encounters. Kangaroo sightings in the United States have been reported since the late 1800s up until very recently. In the early 1970s, numerous kangaroo sightings were reported in the Midwestern states of Illinois, Indiana, and Wisconsin. One of these occurred on October 18, 1974 when a Chicago Police Department dispatcher got a call from a man in the Jefferson Park District, who reported that he was taking out his garbage when he spotted a kangaroo hanging out on his front porch. As in many types of calls of this nature, the police laugh it off and either do not respond or take their time in doing so. Two officers, Patrolman Michael Byrne and Patrolman Leonard Ciagi arrived on the scene at around 3:30 AM and did not find the kangaroo at the residence where it was reported. After searching the neighborhood, they shortly found a five-foot tall, 150 pound kangaroo in a nearby alley located between West Eddy Street and West Cornelia Street just off of North Meade Avenue (coordinates 41°56'40"N, 87°46'46"W). When they approached the creature, it began screaming and

25

growling at them and then it attacked them by trying to punch one of them in the face. The officers managed to strike back with a few blows at its head and then they tried to grab a hold of it and attempted to place it in handcuffs. Their efforts were not successful and the creature really got nasty and retaliated by kicking them. By that time, additional police cruisers arrived on the scene with backup officers. The kangaroo turned and ran down the alley, jumped over a fence, and escaped. Other kangaroo sightings occurred later that afternoon and in the following days at nearby locations. Due to the fact that kangaroos are not native to the United States, doubts began to set in as to whether it was an actual kangaroo. It was placed into a category known as *phantom kangaroos* that are believed to represent an unclassified species. It is believed by some cryptozoologists that many of these are Devil Monkeys,

PAINTSVILLE, KENTUCKY

In 1945, a man from Paintsville, Kentucky had spent the day fishing and he had harvested a mess of catfish. After his day of fishing was done, he returned to his campsite and began cleaning the fish. Suddenly, without warning, a large monkey-like creature tore out of the woods and attacked him. He was unable to fight the vicious creature off and received considerable injures in the scuffle. The man was lucky when the creature broke off from its attack, grabbed up the fisherman's catfish, and then ran back into the woods. Apparently, the creature was a hungry Devil Monkey who merely wanted a free mess of catfish.

WEST POINT, KENTUCKY

There have been many sightings of the Devil Monkey in the Appalachian Mountains of the United States. Included among those sightings is one that took place at West Point, Kentucky one night. Wayman and Marva Morgan were alerted to a commotion taking place outside their house one fateful night back in the early 1970s. Marva Morgan went to a window to look outside and saw a strange figure that resembled a kangaroo-baboon type of creature just a few feet away. The animal had sharp claws and sharp fangs protruding from its mouth and stood on its strong hind legs to a height of five to seven feet. Something had been raiding their garbage cans recently and tonight it was back doing the same routine. Things were different this time, because when it was approached by their dog, the vicious creature tore into the dog and ripped the dog to shreds resulting in its death. The couple ran outside to attempt a rescue of the dog, but the monster had made its getaway. The Devil Monkey did leave something behind—an unmistakably strong, pungent smell.

ALBANY, KENTUCKY

In 1973, the year that I graduated from college, a group of large, black, monkey-like creatures or Devil Monkeys with long tails made their appearance near Albany in Clinton County, Kentucky. In that encounter, they attacked and killed a farmer's livestock. Later a renowned cryptozoologist, Loren Coleman investigated the incident.

In 1978, another farmer, Charles Stern, near Albany reported that a monkey-like creature or Devil Monkey had killed one of his livestock. That farmer fired several shots at the creature which scared it off.

MILTON, KENTUCKY

In 1978, witnesses near Milton in Trimble County, Kentucky came across three creatures, meeting the description of a Devil Monkey, that were walking along a tobacco field in the Ohio River bottoms near Milton. One of these three creatures was larger than the others and began to act violent. It stopped and turned towards the witnesses and it began growling at them until the other two creatures had gotten away. It then took off and followed the others until all of them had disappeared from sight.

DERIDDER, LOUISIANA

Louisiana had its first recorded encounter with one of these strange creatures in 1996. The witness in that case was just the person you would want to report an encounter of this type because he just happened to be a biologist and he was employed as a consultant with a biotechnology firm. Apparently, he was not anxious to admit that he saw such a creature because of the nature of his occupation and therefore he did not wish to have his name published.

The witness was looking out the window of his residence one rainy day when he saw a creature moving around in a nearby field. The field was located on the opposite side of a fence which bordered his piece of land. He thought, at first, that it was a really large dog as it ran and leaped toward him and the fence line. In that case, the animal was first seen running on four legs in a quadupedal fashion. As it approached the fence, which was five feet high, it easily jumped across and landed on his side of the property. At that point, it rose up and stood on two legs in a bipedal fashion. The observer was about ten yards from the strange animal and he realized that what he was looking at was no ordinary creature. It was at least four feet tall and had a rough coat of fur, a long bushy tail, ears that extended upward to a sharp point, yellow eyes, a snout, and thick hair on its face. It had arms like a person and hands with finger-like claws. The witness had heard of a similarly described creature before—the Devil Monkey.

That was not the only incident in Louisiana that was reported in 1996. Another incident occurred in Southwestern Louisiana near the Louisiana-Texas border just south of the City of DeRidder. A motorist was driving along State Highway 12 when she saw a figure lying along the side of the road. One of the first things she might have thought was that it was a pedestrian that had been struck by a moving vehicle. Barbara Mullins looked more closely and realized that it was not human and yet it was a pretty large animal so she stopped to investigate. Closer inspection revealed to her that it might possibly be a dog of very large size—something on the order of a Saint Bernard. The witness also observed that the carcass had a thick coat of dark fur that covered its entire body. As she carefully approached the dead body, she noticed that it more closely resembled a baboon or some perhaps other large monkey-like animal. As she looked at its rear legs, she could see that it had a clearly defined set of feet. A set of pointed ears were present on its head. Excitedly, she just happened to have a camera and managed to maintain her senses and take several photographs which were later examined by the Louisiana Department of Wildlife and Fisheries. The story of her bizarre encounter appeared in the September 25, 1996 weekly edition of the *DeQuincy News*. At the time, it was actually speculated that the creature was a Chupacabra. The *DeRidder Roadkill* case, as it has become known, has been studied by several cryptozoologists and they now believe that the mysterious carcass was that of a Devil Monkey.

DANVILLE, NEW HAMPSHIRE

Danville is a town of population 4400 located in Rockingham County, New Hampshire. On September 9, 2001, it laid claim to its very own sighting of the Devil Monkey. On that night, the Danville fire chief, David Kimball, was driving through town and he was near the intersection of Pleasant Street and Kingson Road when saw the creature. It appeared to be a large primate around three to four feet tall. It displayed a reddish brown coat, a dog-like snout, razor sharp teeth, strong hind legs, and short front legs that terminated in long claws. The creature jumped out into the road, stared at the witness, and then it leaped and hopped on down the road. Eleven other residents of Pleasant Street, including 58 year old Vivian Wicker, were also witnesses to the strange creature and its shrill hooting and howling as it made its getaway into the darkness. After the first sighting, there were at least nine more sightings reported during the following two weeks. The people of Danville were very frightened, especially when they learned that the creature stood as much as eight feet tall. Search parties were sent out several times during the month of September to look for the monster, but their efforts were unsuccessful. Dogs were utilized as part of these search parties, but it was soon discovered that they were refusing to track the creature. It appeared that the creature had finally moved out of town into the nearby mountains. It could sometimes be heard howling at night and the residents of Rockingham County were in a panic about the thought that something which could be very dangerous was lurking near their homes. Several more times, the scary primate turned up in the town of Danville. An NBC-TV news team showed up at one point to cover the story. After some time, the Devil Monkey did not show up again. Some believed that a large monkey had escaped from its captivity at a zoo, a circus, or someone's personal collection of exotic animals.

The Devil Monkey of Rockingham County was not heard from again until fourteen years had passed. In 2015, the local news media published a story that the Devil Monkey had returned. Witnesses reported that they had seen a dangerous looking creature, meeting the same description of the monster that was seen years earlier, dragging the body of a young child or at the very least a doll baby. After some time had passed, no children were actually reported missing, but members of the community of Danville and the outlying areas of Rockingham County were still spooked by the whole affair. Recently, there have been no new sightings of the Devil Monkey and the community feels very fortunate—that is until it surfaces again.

DARE COUNTY, NORTH CAROLINA

In 1997, a woman and her daughter were on vacation and she was en route from her home in Ohio by way of Nashville, Tennessee to Nags Head, North Carolina on the Outer Banks when she had a strange creature sighting. She had been traveling on U. S. Route 158 East from Roanoke Rapids, North Carolina toward Elizabeth City, North Carolina which would normally take her across the Currituck Sound, by way of the Wright Memorial Bridge, onto the Outer Banks. However, due to road construction in the area, she had to take a detour southward near Elizabeth City, North Carolina. After she and her daughter stopped to eat, she resumed driving. She knew that the unexpected detour was going to cause her to arrive at her destination very late that night. She believes that the detour was U. S. Route 17, which carried her about 30 miles southward to another route which crossed over the Albemarle Sound and connected her to U. S. Route 64 East. She then followed that route through the Alligator River National Wildlife Refuge, crossed a bridge over the Alligator River, crossed a bridge over the Croatan Sound, and then arrived on Roanoke Island. One final bridge across Roanoke Sound took her to her final destination at her vacation home in Nags Head.

It was around 2:30 AM and the roadway was dark as she, with her daughter asleep in the back seat, traveled along toward her destination. She did not know her exact location, but she knew that she had just gone past a "Red Wolf Crossing" sign along the side of the road just minutes before. That would have placed her in the Alligator River National Wildlife Refuge because the Red Wolf warning signs were placed along a ten mile stretch of U. S. Route 64 back in 1987 when the federal government reintroduced the Red Wolf (Canus rufus) species to that area and created the Red Wolf Recovery Area. While driving along that stretch of road, a large, black creature with short fur jumped out in front of her car. The creature was about six feet tall, stood on its hind legs, was well muscled, had a blunt nose shorter than a canine and kind of like a cat, had pointed ears, and it had a long thin tail. In some ways the animal was cat-like with large legs shaped like those of a cat or dog. She later commented that the creature had a torso much like a man. The creature may have been on all four legs when she approached and it stood in front of her car as she braked to a stop. It stood in front of her headlights for a moment and then it took a power leap and jumped completely across both lanes of the road. It is thought that a jump of that distance was at least 18 feet. The witness stated that it was not a Red Wolf or even a Black Wolf, but that it was something else. She discussed the encounter with the U. S. Fish and Wildlife Service and they led her in a different direction by trying to convince her that what she saw was a dog, a feral dog, or a hybrid wolf-dog. The witness did not go along with that theory. Her final decision was that she had seen an animal matching the description of a Devil Monkey.

AUTHORS NOTE: This sighting has often been referred to as a Roanoke, Virginia sighting but the Roanoke in this incident was most likely Roanoke Rapids, North Carolina along Route 158 or Roanoke Island, North Carolina along U. S. Route 64 near the

Outer Banks. The witness mentions passing "Lost Colony" signs which are associated with a late 16th century English settlement of 117 people that disappeared under mysterious circumstances from Roanoke Island. That piece of history is reenacted each summer on the original settlement site during regular presentations of "The Lost Colony" outdoor theatrical drama.

LICKING COUNTY, OHIO

A local sheriff's department employee recently recalled an incident that occurred On January 15, 1984 in Licking County, Ohio when she and a friend were on a cheerleading squad. They were headed to a basketball game at Licking Valley High School where they would be cheering that night. They were driving north on Brownsville Road (County Route 668), which is mostly bordered by farmland and open fields on both sides of the road. They had entered a one mile stretch of road through an area of dense forest and brush, which lies just before the bridge across Clay Lick Creek about one mile south of State Route 16. The Licking River borders that particular forest to the north. It was around 5:30 PM that evening and the temperature was around

40°F even though it had been sunny earlier that afternoon.

They were just cruising along when they came upon something large and hairy setting in the middle of the road directly in their path of travel. The creature appeared to be a large baboon-like animal with light brown, caramel colored hair. The creature looked at them and its face was ape-like. As they closed in on the creature, it was too late to veer off the road in order to avoid a collision because they were afraid of running into the creek. At the last moment, the creature seemed to have jumped out of the way and the car did not collide with it.

This incident was reported on the Bigfoot Field Researchers Organization (BFRO) site about 20 years after it occurred as a possible Bigfoot sighting. The witness has later learned that there had been sighting reports of a similar nature from other witnesses around that same time frame. The creature's resemblance to a baboon, the caramel colored hair, and its ability to jump out of the way of an oncoming car have caused me to make a decision that the incident involving this creature was more than likely a Devil Monkey sighting.

DUNKINSVILLE, OHIO

Dunkinsville is an unincorporated community in Adams County, Ohio. It is geographically located in the Appalachian Mountains to the west of Ohio's Shawnee State Forest. The area is endowed with a sort of magic because not far away is the mysterious Serpent Mound and there is also a nearby church with an image of Christ burned into the surface of its door. At nearby Peach Mountain is a GE Testing Facility where a number of strange things such as Bigfoot sightings and UFO encounters have occurred. However, the strangeness does not end there. On June 26, 1997, Dunkinsville was also the site of an encounter with a strange monkey-like creature that was believed to be a Devil Monkey.

The incident took place at the residence of Debbie Cross, which was situated about five miles northeast of town. The property is described as a wooded ridge near Peach Mountain. On that particular night, shortly after midnight, Cross was in her living room watching television when she was alerted to a disturbance outside her house. Her dogs were barking frantically, so she went to the door to see what was causing the ruckus. She flipped on a bright porch light and saw something moving near a pond that was located in her front yard. About 30 feet away, she was able to clearly see a strange creature about five feet tall that was covered with gray fur about one to two inches in length. It displayed large dark eyes that were recessed into its face and it had short rounded ears (some accounts say pointed). The animal had a short tail and long arms. The animal watched her for a few seconds and then moved on toward the opposite end of the pond. Its method of locomotion consisted of a kind of hopping or skipping motion combine with walking on its hind legs while occasionally supporting itself with its arms by resting its knuckles on the ground. During the time that all of this was taking place, the animal emitted a gurgling or growling sound. The dogs took off in pursuit as the creature moved away from the house, but Cross was able to call them back. As the creature move farther away, it followed a barbed wire fence until it gradually disappeared from her sight. Later, she heard a screeching sound and she believes that it came from the creature—a creature that she believes was a Devil Monkey.

IRONTON, OHIO

Ironton is a city in Lawrence County, Ohio located in the southern part of the state along the Ohio River. Its name is derived from the words "iron town" because the area was a major producer of pig iron between 1850 and 1890. More than 90 iron furnaces operated there by the end of the 1800s because of the areas rich iron deposits which were located north of the city. One of the oldest iron furnaces, the Vesuvius Furnace, was built there in 1833. The remains of that furnace still stand near the Lake Vesuvius Recreational Area in the Wayne National Forest about 6 miles north of Ironton. It was named after the Italian volcano, Vesuvius, because of the fiery, hot temperatures needed to smelt the iron ore. Ironton also happens to be 36 miles southwest of Point Pleasant where Mothman was first sighted in 1966.

According to stories that have been preserved down through the years, a devil-like creature appeared in the area near the Vesuvius Furnace on a daily basis around the year 1875. The creature began to harass the furnace workers, the miners in the nearby iron mines, and others who were associated with the industry. The iron furnace employees worked for low wages and were paid with company script that could be spent only in the company store. When the creature began to appear, it is no surprise that the workers felt that the Devil himself had climbed out of a hot iron furnace just to torture them a little more. The creature was said to block the path of the workers while they were en route to work at their respective job locations.

THE VESUVIUS IRON FURNACE AT IRONTON, OHIO
PUBLIC DOMAIN PHOTO FROM WIKIPEDIA

According to the March 11, 1985 edition of the *Ironton Register*, a resident of nearby Long Creek was riding home when he saw the creature in the vicinity of the Vesuvius Furnace. The thing suddenly came out of the bushes and made its appearance and then it quickly went back into the bushes. He was unable to give a really good description of it because he did not recover quickly enough from the shock. The description he gave, which was a simple one, stated that it had a "thin body, low squatty legs, and a long black tail." It was "unlike any animal he ever saw before." The description given by the witness indicates that it was a kind of animal and not the Devil himself as it was thought by the superstitious iron workers that had never seen such a manifestation before.

The problem with the so-called Devil continued until it reached a point that it was severely affecting daily operations at the iron furnace, so the company owner called in a priest to try and negotiate with it. According to the stories that have been handed down, the priest asked the creature, "What in the name of God do you want?" The creature did not answer the priest, but it never showed up again so the problem was solved.

The stories of the creature that have been handed down from generation to generation, along with the description given by the witness in the *Ironton Register* news article, are enough to cause one to suspect that the encounters with this creature could quite possibly have been one of the earliest sightings of the Devil Monkey.

OKLAHOMA

Sometime in 1975, three Oklahoma outdoorsmen ran into a strange creature which they described as being a large monkey. They were in a large open area when they first spotted the critter. As the three men stared at the creature, it emitted a low growling sound that was enough to make their hair stand on end. The three men, Anthony Ketchum, Steve Ketchum, and a friend named Allen Herrin first saw the hair covered, man-sized creature with a long tail moving around near them at a distance, but then it turned and started hopping right toward them. It didn't take any additional encouragement for them to make a quick exit and get out of its way. The incident was later studied and it is believed to have been a Devil Monkey encounter.

CHESTER COUNTY, PENNSYLVANIA

Two communities were the scene of an unusual monster sighting that occurred during the 1930s around 30 miles west of Philadelphia in Southeastern Pennsylvania. Eagle, Pennsylvania is an unincorporated community located in the Upper Uwchian Township of Chester County. The coordinates of that location are 40°04'41"N, 75°41'16"W. It was there that a local resident had a strange creature sighting on January 21, 1932. While out walking, he ran onto an ugly, scary monster that he described as half-man and half-beast. The creature was covered in dark hair and was observed walking on all fours. It wasn't long afterward that another sighting took place 2.5 miles away near Dorlan, Pennsylvania located in the East Brandywine Township of Chester County. The coordinates of that location are 40°02'52"N, 75°42'58"W. Two employees of a local nursery, James McCandless of Lansdowne and Josiah Hoopes of West Chester, were working in the woods around Dorlan when they had a scary encounter by running head-on into the same or a similar creature. The men described the monster as being neither man nor beast and they said that it moved about by a combination of walking and leaping.

McCandless realized that this was no ordinary creature and that it might be quite dangerous, so he organized an armed search party to seek it out. They searched the area far and wide and were unable to find the creature or any of its tracks. The *Dorlan Devil*, as it became known, seemed to have completely vanished from the area—for the time being.

The monster did not show itself again until five years later on July 28, 1937. Cydney Ladley, a local worker in a paper mill at Downingtown, was traveling in his car from Dorlan to Milford Mills. Accompanying him as passengers in the car was his wife, Mrs. Ladley, along with her friend, Mrs. Chester Smith. While traveling along the road to Milford Mills on that warm July night, something jumped out into the road in front of their car. The creature, illuminated by their headlights, was described as being like a kangaroo with long black hair and eyes like large red saucers. The creature was able to jump clear across the road in one leap and then disappear into a swamp on the opposite side of the road. The three witnesses were engulfed in fear as the creature passed before them, but it took a few more seconds for it to really sink in. Mr. Ladley jammed down on the accelerater and didn't let any grass grow under the tires as sped toward the safety of home. Later, Ladley revealed that it was the large, burning, red eyes which had chilled him to the bone. Immediately, after the encouter along the road to Milford Mills, Ladley contacted some of his friends and organized a search party. The men brought their guns and hunting dogs and entered the area where the monster was last seen. The search continued for hours until everyone was worn clear out. They were unsucessful in their efforts to turn up any trace of the devil monster.

Both James Candless and Cydney Ladley were familiar with the wildlife of the area and they claimed that what they had seen along the Dorlan-Milford Mills Road did not remotely resemble anything they had ever seen before. Both men were asked, at the time of their encounters, if what they had seen could have simply been a deer, but they knew what a deer looked like and the creature was definitely not one. Many of the locals thought that it was all a hoax and they made fun of the witnesses when the story came out in the local newspapers. One such article appeared in the July 28, 1937 edition of the *Downington Archive*. Other sightings followed, including one on February 13, 1939 when another creature of the same description was seen by Sylvester Scott near Coatesville,

Pennsylvania. In Southern Chester County, there is an area called Devil's Woods in which creatures of the same type are known to inhabit. The description of the monsters described in the above narrative has lead myself and others to think that these sightings in Chester County, Pennsylvania have all been encounters with the Devil Monkey.

As a final note, between 1964 and 1978, the State of Pennsylvania purchased 1705 acres of property in that area to become the Marsh Creek State Park. A 535 acre water impoundment, Marsh Creek Lake, was created to solve a water supply problem in Chester County, control flooding, and provide recreational opportunities. Farmland around Milford Mills was flooded to create the lake and in doing so, the area of the sighting is now under water. In doing so, the Devil Monkey's lair may have been eliminated.

SOUTH PITTSBURG, TENNESSEE

It was in January of 1934 that several unusual encounters with a strange beast occurred within a five day interval at South Pittsburg, Tennessee. This new animal could leap long distances of 20 feet and travel with lightning speed across the terrain. One of the witnesses was Reverend W. J. Hancock who watched it run across a farmer's field. Other witnesses said that it had attacked and killed German Shepherd police dogs leaving behind only the head and shoulders. Several water fowl such as ducks and geese were also devoured. Another witness claimed that he saw it crossing a field while carrying a sheep under one of its arms. A group of armed farmers formed a search party and they followed the animal's tracks which led to a cave up in the hills. Not one member of the group was willing to enter the cave and since they were unable to find the creature, they discontinued their search. The whole story was in the national news and was followed closely by reporters. The mysterious creature was labeled by some as a marsupial-like primate because in some ways, it resembled a kangaroo while at the same time it had the characteristics of an ape. At the time, many of these sightings were reported as carnivorous "killer kangaroo" sightings. However, actual kangaroos are herbivores and not carnivores. Loren Coleman, a leading expert in the world of cryptozoology, believes that these critters were actually Devil Monkeys.

BELLOWS FALLS, VERMONT

Bellows Falls is an incorporated village located within the Town of Rockingham, Windham County, Vermont. It is located four miles north of Westminster, Vermont. On Sunday, August 21, 2016, several reports began to come in to the Bellows Falls Police Department that a monkey-like creature had been sighted in the area. The next day, a man reported to the police that a brown monkey had crossed the road in front of his car on Back Westminster Road where it intersects with Vermont State Route 121 near Interstate 91. That sighting location is 1.75 miles east of the Vermont and New Hampshire state line at coordinates 43°07'27"N, 72°28'18"W. The story of the encounter was featured in a news broadcast on TV station NBC-5 from Burlington, Vermont.

The creature was thought to be a small Sasquatch by one Bigfoot site. However, the creature had a tail which brought into play the theory that it was an actual monkey that had escaped captivity. Monkeys are not native to the United States and there are generally strict laws governing the possession of one. In the state of Vermont and New Hampshire, a permit is required to own a monkey and that is only if it is intended to be used as a service animal. Another alternative to consider, the one which I have chosen, is that the creature was actually a Devil Monkey.

SALTVILLE, VIRGINIA

Another well known sighting occurred in 1959 at Saltville, a small town in Smyth and Washington Counties of Virginia. The Boyd family owned a local restaurant and they had agreed to operate a concession stand for a three-day church activity that was set to begin the next morning. They were in need of certain supplies which required them to get up early and drive to Saltville in order that they could return and be back before the activities began later that morning. They were en route before 3:00 AM that morning and things had gone well until they made a wrong turn and found themselves driving along a narrow mountainous road in a desolate area. As they rounded a turn, they could see a high embankment on the right side of the road. Suddenly, they saw a movement and they slowed almost to a stop because they thought that it was a deer about to run across the road in front of them. A daughter, Pauline Boyd, recalled the frightening experience that followed as it was later told to her by her parents. An animal leaped off the embankment toward their car and thrust its face right up against the passenger side window. Pauline Boyd stated that her mother reluctantly got a close-up view of the animal. She described the fur or hair on the monster as light colored with a white blaze of hair on its neck and stomach. It stood and walked on two, large, muscular legs and it displayed a pair of short, front legs. The scary part was that the animal, which resembled an ape or baboon, began to chase them and attack their car. She stated that her father stepped on the accelerator and sped away from the animal. As soon as he had gained some ground on the animal, he stopped the car and stepped out with a pistol with the intent of taking a shot at the animal. Her mother convinced him to get back in the car because she was afraid that the monster would catch up with them and that the bullets would not stop it. Her father jumped back into the car and sped on down the road toward Saltville. Upon their arrival in town, an inspection of their car revealed that the fierce animal attack had left deep scar marks in the paint on the passenger side door of their car. The scar marks were configured in rows of three which gave evidence that he creature had three claws on each foot. They said that the animal, even though it bore resemblance to both a kangaroo and a monkey, was not a kangaroo, a dog, or a bear as some people tried to suggest. Their daughter, Pauline Boyd, believes that her parents had an unfriendly encounter with a Devil Monkey.

That was not the end of the creature's presence in Saltville. Two days later, in the same area, two nurses were driving home from work early in the morning when their car was attacked in a similar manner by a creature meeting the same description and resembling a baboon. The animal managed to tear the canvas top off of their convertible as it tried to get at the two passengers. The driver and passenger were very thankful that the vicious creature was unsuccessful and they were able to make a clean get-a-way in what was left of their car. A search party was organized and members of the group took along their hunting dogs in pursuit of the animal. Once the party began to follow the creature's trail and its scent was picked up, the dogs began to behave strangely and refused to go any farther.

A third sighting in the Saltville area occurred sometime during the 1990s. A couple had recently purchased a piece of property with a mobile home in the area to be use for weekends, holidays, and vacations. On that particular weekend, the couple and their two children were en route to Saltville for the weekend. They were traveling in their truck along a quiet highway that runs parallel to Interstate 81. As they approached the top of a hill, a large creature ran out into the roadway and forced the man to apply his brakes to avoid a collision. The creature was down on all four legs and its front legs were shorter than its larger and much stronger looking rear legs. All four feet had sharp claws. It stood about three feet high when they saw it, but if it had stood up, they estimated that it would have been at least five feet tall. It was covered in gray hair or fur with a long nose and pointed ears.

The creature crossed the highway, jumped across a ditch line, ran through the weeds, and then it hurdled a fence that ran along the road. The couple believes that the creature met the description of a Devil Monkey.

In 1973, a man was driving State Route 16 northward from Marion, Virginia to Tazewell, Virginia. The straight line distance between the two towns is 20 miles. He was crossing the mountain on the Marion side, which is around 12 to 14 miles east of Saltville, when he encountered a creature he believes to have been a Devil Monkey. He was motoring up the winding mountain road with his window rolled down and his arm hanging out the window. Both sides of the road were heavily wooded in that area. When he heard a noise outside the car to his left, he turned and looked in that direction just in time to see a vicious creature rushing from the side of the road toward his car. The creature tried to grab his arm prompting him to jerk it back inside the car and lay on the accelerator. He was so shaken up that he never slowed down or looked back until he arrived at his destination.

Several out-of-towners from Goochland, Virginia that were hunting in the Saltville area recently claimed that they heard strange sounds, described as sounding like a monkey, coming from the forest around where they were hunting. They have hunted all their lives and have never heard anything make that kind of sound in the woods before. They have not returned to the Saltville area since that time and they do not intend to do so anytime in the future. Those visitors from Goochland know firsthand a little something about the Devil Monkey.

GOOCHLAND, VIRGINIA

For the last 40 years, I have had the opportunity to travel Interstate 64 through Virginia and I have been curious about the origin of strange sounding names assigned to several towns along the way. I learned that *Stuarts Draft* was named after a man named Stuart, while "draft" may have referred to the document or deed that was drafted—it is also a term for a river or stream. The town of *Mechanicsville* is derived from the fact that a number of skilled tradesmen or "mechanics" lived in that "ville" or village. *Short Pump* is a town that received its name from a tavern that had an outside water pump with a short handle. *Cold Harbor* is the location of a Civil War battlefield and years ago, a tavern was originally located there. The term "harbor" commonly refers to a place of shelter for a boat. In this case the shelter was an inn or tavern and it was rumored that the owner of the tavern served cold food. *Goochland* is the county seat of Goochland County, Virginia and was named after a Lieutenant Governor by the name of Goochland.

Recently, while on a trip to the Outer Banks, North Carolina to investigate a *Goatman* legend, I checked out Goochland which is located along

Interstate 64 East at exit 159 and south on U. S. Route 522. I learned that there is a legend, going back 40 years, of a strange animal that stalks the woods around the town of Goochland. Stories of the animal have circulated to the extent that the creature has evolved into a legend—that of the Devil Monkey. However, there is a drawback. It seems that most of the local citizens really don't want to talk about it. However, something related to the Devil Monkey must be going on in that town. I found out that in 2012, the Jandzinski family opened an ice cream establishment right downtown near the courthouse square and named it the *Devil Monkey Ice Cream Parlor*. Unfortunately, they recently closed the iconic business much to the disappointment of the local connoisseurs of fine ice cream.

In the November and December of 2010, several local citizens claimed that they saw the strange creature in downtown Goochland near the Goochland County Courthouse Square historic district. The historic Grace Episcopal Church and its spooky old graveyard are also located nearby. There are a number of businesses located in that area also.

According to witnesses in one of the sightings, the creature stood up on all four legs with it front legs being much shorter than its rear legs. It had pointed ears, a pronounced nose, and a long, furry tail. All of these descriptions meet those of the Devil Monkey. Witnesses claimed that the monster behaved in a menacing manner by showing its teeth and producing somewhat of a growling sound. Then it just ran off in a leaping fashion.

Two other witnesses saw the creature, or one like it, a few miles away on the south end of Rock Castle Road (County Route 600) in 2010. The animal had an ape-like appearance and it stood up and walked across the road right in front of their vehicle. These same witnesses saw the creature again, nearly four years later, in June of 2014. The witness was traveling westward on County Route 6 toward Goochland, and when they were about 1.25 miles from town, the creature came out of the woods on the north side of the road and began to cross the road toward the river on the left. The witness slammed on his brakes and the creature reversed its path and returned back across the road and into the woods from which it came. All of these witnesses believe that they saw a Devil Monkey, but very few of them want to talk about it because they don't like being the object of ridicule.

Other sightings around that time occurred near a local law firm on November 17, near the local high school on November 26, at the intersection of County Route 632 and County Route 634 on December 1, at nearby Oilville on December 3, at Riddles Bridge Road on December 4, and again at the Goochland Courthouse Square on December 7. Some witnesses say that the creature somewhat resembled a kangaroo. Many of the locals were glad of school closings due to snow around that time because they were afraid to have children out waiting on the school bus with such a creature around. The Devil Monkey sightings became the talk of the town during that period of time.

The Goochland County Sheriff's office reported that they believed the whole affair to be a hoax. However, the general opinion among the local citizenry is that the witnesses were good, solid, reliable people with no reason to make up such a story. TV station NBC-12 out of nearby Richmond did a news story on the whole affair.

POINT PLEASANT, WEST VIRGINIA

Recently, I returned to my hometown of Point Pleasant, West Virginia in Mason County to do a little research. I have found myself returning there quite often in search of answers, because that place has turned out to be a treasure trove of really weird things. As most of you already know, Point Pleasant was the scene of the famous encounter with Mothman, back in 1966, at the old TNT Area. From time to time, the area has played host to other strange entities including Bigfoot, Sheepsquatch, and Dogman. At one point, it was literally a hotbed for UFO activity. Now, I have returned there to see if there might be a Devil Monkey connection.

It was a nice day when I drove into Point Pleasant with the intention of checking out a location which I had not had a chance to visit when I was growing up there. My main interest that day was an area up State Route 62, just north of the city limits, on Lucas Lane where it crosses the railroad tracks. I arrived at my destination, parked in a graveled area near the railway, and stepped out of my vehicle to look around. The old Cecil Lucas farm, the object of my attention that day, lies on the opposite side of the tracks next to the Ohio River. Oldtown Creek, which flows through the TNT Area, also passes through this farm and empties into the Ohio River nearby. The old Lucas Farm is 1.2 miles north of the old abandoned Marietta Manufacturing Company and the secretive Defense Logistics Agency. It is 3.4 miles south of the famous TNT Area. There are also several prehistoric Indian burial sites located nearby. All of these features add to the high strangeness of the whole area. I took several photographs while I was at the location and explored the area along the railroad tracks in both directions. I didn't find anything unusual on that day, because it all happened over 50 years ago.

RAILROAD CROSSING AT OLD CECIL LUCAS FARM
ON LUCAS LANE NORTH OF POINT PLEASANT
PHOTO BY AUTHOR

Around the time that the Mothman appeared in the TNT Area, a number of animal mutilation reports were made. Farmers reported that they were finding dead cows with the carcasses turned inside out. Soon, cats and dogs were included in mutilation reports that came in. Since the Mothman had just announced its arrival, many blamed the winged creature with everything weird that was taking place.

With everything that was happening around Point Pleasant, it is not surprising that people began keeping a protective eye on their pets and that local farmers in the predominately rural farming community of Mason County began keeping a closer check on their livestock. Cecil E. and Mildred E. Lucas owned a farm along the northern border of Point Pleasant, just south of the well known C. C. Lewis Farm. In November of 1966, around the time of the Mothman sightings at Point Pleasant, Cecil Lucas was at home one evening when he heard dogs barking outside his house. He got up and went outside to see what the commotion was all about and found that something was happening out in his pasture field. Near an oilfield pump jack, next to some oil storage tanks, he saw three strange looking creatures with dark fur. He was unable to determine their exact color because it was too dark. The creatures switched back and forth from walking on four legs at times to walking on their hind legs. When the creatures noticed that he was approaching, they rose up onto their hind legs and ran away into the darkness. After that night, Mr. Lucas never saw them again.

SCENE WHERE THREE STRANGE CREATURES WERE
SEEN NEAR OIL TANKS AT LUCAS FARM IN 1966
PHOTO BY AUTHOR

In the days that followed, not far away on Jericho Road, there were also several sightings of similar creatures. Those creatures were referred to, by Mary Hyre, as the *Jericho Road Man-Bears*.

If you are not already familiar, Mary Hyre was a reporter for *The Athens Messenger* who originally covered the Mothman story and also had a run-in with the mysterious *Men in Black*.

In the past, in other books that I have written, I have not forgotten this particular incident and I have attributed it to a possible encounter with several notable creature types including Bigfoot, Sheepsquatch, and Dogman. Since the entities were seen alternating from walking on all fours (quadrupedal) to walking on two legs (bipedal), I am now considering another option. I believe that the three creatures seen 50 years ago on the Lucas Farm might possibly have been Devil Monkeys. Therefore, I have included that encounter in this book.

LINCOLN COUNTY, WEST VIRGINIA

The State of West Virginia is right in the middle of Appalachia and that is just the place for a really weird creature to make its debut. Appalachian folklore is based upon a combination of European, Native American, and Biblical influence. Much of the Appalachian folklore has its origins in English, Scottish, and Irish fairy tales because of the European background of the early settlers to the region. The Native American Cherokee folklore has influenced the Appalachian storytelling in regard to the characteristics and depiction of local animals. Hunting tales involving local animals have also contributed to the local folklore. Stories about strange creatures such as the 1966 appearance of the Mothman at Point Pleasant have become part of the local culture and have grown to worldwide proportions.

A resident of West Virginia, who grew up in Lincoln County has recalled a story told to him by his grandfather when he was young. His grandfather was a retired station agent for the Chesapeake and Ohio Railroad and was in charge of the railroad station at McCorkle, West Virginia during the early 1940s. In those days, the railroad was a major means of American transportation. Trains carried passengers and cargo between small communities and major population centers across the United States. In West Virginia, trains hauled coal and timber out of the mining and timbering towns to industrial centers all over the country. During the early 1940s, World War II was in full swing and the railroads were busy hauling coal out of southern counties such as Lincoln, Boone, Logan, Mingo, and McDowell. Therefore, railroad repair crews were kept busy maintaining the tracks between the station at McCorkle, West Virginia in Lincoln County and Julian, West Virginia in Boone County. That section of tracks runs along the Little Coal River and it is not more than six miles in length, but in those days the area was extremely isolated from civilization.

According to a story, as told by the retired station agent, workers along that stretch of tracks began telling him about an unidentified animal that had been scaring the workers and creating havoc for them. The creature was ape-like and it swung through trees as it screamed and shrieked at the workers. Soon, the situation escalated when several workers had to conduct some intensive labor along a stretch of track about a mile or so south of McCorkle.

One night, a repair crew that consisted of a foreman and three workers had to stay on the job about two miles south of McCorkle. They were spending the night in a caboose that was parked on a siding along the tracks when they had a scary encounter. They were awakened during the night to the sound of something scratching on the side of the caboose. Upon closer inspection, one of the workers was looking out a window when he saw a vicious looking creature with sharp teeth scraping on the windows with some really sharp claws. The worker carelessly went outside without thinking of the possible consequences. What he witnessed was a large ape-like creature with a dog-like face and large teeth still gouging at the window. The creature then began to shriek and scream like a mountain lion, except that was not what it was—it was something else. The worker reacted in a manner consistent with what you might expect from a West Virginian who always comes prepared. He promptly went back inside the caboose and retrieved some firepower in the form of a loaded shotgun. The animal was still trying to dig his way into the caboose when the worker fired one round at it. The creature let out a scream and ran off into the nearby woods. The workers brought out a kerosene railroad lantern and commenced to searching the animal's path of departure for any signs of blood. They were unable to find any trace of the creature or its blood, so they assumed that the shotgun blast had missed the animal.

During the next few years, there were sightings of the creature by passengers riding on the train and from railroad workers working along the tracks. Two local residents of the area reported seeing a large, vicious, dog-faced, killer monkey moving around the railroad community. After World War II was over, reports of the creature dwindled to nothing and it was never seen again. That area of the state may have been a little isolated during those days, but news reports still spread of other creature sightings of a similar nature that had taken place elsewhere in Appalachia during the 1930s. Those sightings and the ones in the McCorkle and Julian areas of West Virginia are now being chalked up to encounters with the Devil Monkey.

NEW BRUNSWICK, CANADA

On June 5, 1979, a three to four foot tall creature with strong hind legs, small front legs with paws, a long tail, and grayish-brown fur was sighted in the town of Nelson-Miramichi in the province of New Brunswick, Canada. On that date around 3:30 AM, a security guard by the name of Roy Hanley was working at the Acadia Forest Products Mill when he saw the creature up close to within ten feet of where he was standing. The creature was just as shocked as the guard and after they stared at each other, the creature basically leaped away and disappeared. As in some of these types of sightings, the security guard believed that the animal was a kangaroo-like creature due to its strong hind legs and the way it leaped about. In this sighting, the creature was given droopy ears rather than sharp pointed ones. This sighting and other similar ones have been chalked up to being Devil Monkey sightings. Later in that same summer, a taxi driver and his passenger also saw a similar creature near the same mill. Other witnesses eventually claimed that they also saw the same animal.

NOVA SCOTIA, CANADA

Nova Scotia is a large island and also a province of Canada. In 1984, a creature meeting the description of a Devil Monkey was seen by a George Messinger near Lochiel Lake in Antigonish County, Nova Scotia. It was about three feet tall with short front legs that were held close to its body and large, strong hind legs. This creature was described as being kangaroo-like. In this sighting, the creature was given a head and snout shaped like that of a deer. Other sightings such as this one soon occurred in Nova Scotia near the city of Halifax and the municipality of Guysborough.

BRITISH COLUMBIA, CANADA

In 1969, the same year that I graduated from high school and departed for college, a creature much like the ones described above was making its appearance in the Canadian Province of British Columbia. A large monkey-like animal with a long tail and feet with three toes was reported to be stalking the forests near Mamquam. That scary, creepy entity, thought to be another Devil Monkey, left behind evidence in the form of its three-toed tracks.

STAFFORDSHIRE COUNTY, ENGLAND

It was in England, in the year 1879, that a gentleman had an encounter with a yet to be identified, living creature or perhaps some unworldly, paranormal entity. On January 31, 1879, the impending witness had driven a horse and cart from Ranton in Staffordshire County to another village near Newport in Shropshire County for the purpose of transporting luggage for someone who was being relocated to a new residence.

It was getting late when his mission was accomplished and he was forced to begin his trip home on that cold, winter night. He was traveling a road which would soon carry him across a bridge spanning the Birmingham and Liverpool Canal. That bridge, referred to as the High Bridge No. 39, can still be seen today about one mile southeast of the Staffordshire village of Woodseaves along highway A519 where it crosses the Shropshire Union Canal (coordinates 52°49′55″N, 02°18′48″W). The gentleman, along with his horse and cart, arrived at the bridge sometime around 10:00 PM and that is when an unforeseen, terrifying event unfolded.

Suddenly, a large, black, monkey-like beast with shiny white eyes came running out of the dense forest along the side of the road and jumped upon the man's horse. Not only was the man frightened, but the creature spooked the horse and it broke into a run. The bewildered driver tried to maintain his senses and he managed to take his long whip and crack the beast with it. That is when the man realized that the beast was something of a ghostly entity because the whip just passed right through its body. The shaken driver completely lost his whip and it fell to the road as the horse, which was already tired from a long day, ran like crazy until it reached the village of Woodseaves one mile up the road. Somewhere along the line, the creature must have jumped off, but the man didn't know when because he had lost control of both the horse and his mind. The man, shaking all over, rolled into the nearest English pub where he downed several tankards of brew while he told those who gathered around him about being attacked by the big black ghost-like monkey with brightly shining eyes. Those at the establishment, who would have had to pass across that bridge on the way home that night, elected to spend the rest of the night right where they were.

During the remaining part of the late 1800s, the beast was seen many more times near the high bridge over the Shropshire Union Canal. The beast, which has been considered to be either a cryptid or a paranormal entity, is undoubtedly the best representative of a Devil Monkey that the United Kingdom has to offer. It seems to meet most of the qualifications. I am not sure how one could amass so much information on this creature, but Nick Redfern has written an entire book, titled *Man-Monkey*, which is recommended reading for anyone interested in that entity.

HIMALAYA MOUNTAINS, NEPAL

In June of 1953, Dr. George Moore, MD, MPH was working for the United States Public Health Service, serving in Nepal, a country which separates India from Tibet. He, along with his wife, Constance and daughter were living in Kathmandu, the capital of Nepal during their stay. The country of Nepal had been closed pretty much to foreigners from 1816 up until 1951, but now they were accepting the advice and assistance of outside experts as related to health and other matters. At the time, they were concerned with an epidemic of Typhus, a disease caused by the Rickettsia bacteria that was spreading among the Sherpas in the higher elevations of the Himalaya Mountains. Dr. George Moore was accompanied by Dr. George T. Brooks Ph.D., an entomologist, on that mission into the Himalayas. After their mission was complete, they began the return trip back down the slopes of the Himalayas to Kathmandu. In the high altitudes, at 17,000 feet, they had dealt with heavy snow, but now the monsoon rains from India were moving northward toward them. They had been accompanied by a caravan of Sherpas that carried heavy backpacks of supplies and medicine on the way up the mountain and on the return trip back down. The trail back down the slopes of the Himalayas was treacherous and they had just negotiated the last of the high altitude sections of the trail at Gosainkund Pass. Dr. Moore and Dr. Brooks were anxious to get on down the remaining 28 mile stretch of mountain slope to the foot of the Himalayas and their home at Kathmandu. They moved on ahead and left the caravan behind them on the trail. The two missionaries of health were making their way along a section of muddy trail when they decide to stop for a moment, giving Brooks a moment to knock a leech off of his boot and Moore to light up his pipe. Suddenly, they both realized that something was wrong when they saw movement in a heavy thicket nearby. They were standing on the trail with a bank which dropped sharply off below them and an incline which rose steeply behind them. The only protection available was a huge rock along the trail, so they quickly moved into position behind it. The only other thing in their favor, beside the rock, was the fact that each of them was armed with a handgun, a legendary Smith and Wesson .38 revolver, and they didn't waste any time drawing them from their holsters. Then, whatever it was that was out there, let out a murderously, shrill scream that came from directly in front of them. It was followed up by another vocalization which came from somewhere right behind them. More screams came in unison from all around them. They realized that they were surrounded by something very dangerous, but they didn't what or how many. The questions that were racing through their minds as to what was out there were soon answered when an ugly, terrifying face poked its way out of some nearby bushes and stared directly at them. The face had gray-colored skin, dark black eyebrows, a wide mouth, big yellow teeth, and really mean looking yellow eyes that homed in on them. Moore thought he knew in an instance what it was. He had heard the Sherpas tell many tales, while setting around their campfires, about the *Snow Beast*, the *Yeti*, the *Abominable Snowman*, or whatever you want to call it. He had heard the stories of Sherpas that had run up against the creature and not lived to tell about it. In those instances, the only thing left behind was a mutilated body and large tracks leading from the crime scene. There were tales of some who had survived an attack and made it back to civilization to tell their story. Moore and Brooks had a more pressing situation at that point as they counted seven of the creatures as they stepped out of the wilderness into the open. One monster appeared to be the leader of the group.

Even though an attack was imminent, Moore took inventory of what the largest monster looked like. It was around five feet tall, it partly crouched down on its hind legs, it had hands or fingers that terminated in long, sharp claws, its body was thin with shaggy gray hair, and it showed them its teeth which revealed two, long, sharp fangs sticking out from under its thick lips. The creature seemed to walk, bent over, like a prehistoric caveman. Everything was ape-like in appearance and the two men were sure that they were experiencing a first-hand encounter with a Yeti. Then, both men noticed something that set the creature apart from being a Yeti. The monster featured a long tail—these creatures were obviously something different. Time was running out as the creatures advanced toward them and the two men had to make a quick decision. If they shot one of the monsters, the rest of group might go crazy and retaliate with a vengeance against them. Another problem was that the Sherpa coolies, as they arrived along the trail later, might take it as the killing of one of their gods and they would be angry. Moore and Brooks decided to act immediately and fire a couple of rounds. As they drew the hammers back on their weapons, the mechanical clicking sound caused the creatures to momentarily pause. Then, the two men each fired a round simultaneously. The creatures jumped back and they retreated back into their hiding places. The men each fired a second round and then a third. Moore and Brooks knew that the creatures had retreated, but only for the time being. The two men decide to wait the situation out until the caravan of Sherpas arrived. They had a theory that the creatures would not attack such a large party of men, so they laid down on the large rock to wait the situation out. Out in the bushes, they could hear some ape chatter and one of the monsters would occasionally poke its head out through the branches to see if they were still there. Brooks lit a cigarette and smoked it while Moore played with the hammer on his gun. The ape chatter finally began to slow down and they were wondering if the beasts were planning their second attack. After a while, the chatter suddenly picked back up and suddenly became louder. It was beginning to get dark and the men knew that something was about to happen. They noticed movement advancing toward them in the foggy mist along the trail and they prepared to do battle with the monsters. Then, they realized that it was not the creatures approaching, but that it was the caravan of Sherpas who had finally caught up with them. The leader of the caravan stated that he had heard shots being fired and had ordered the rest of the party to step it up and get there as soon as possible. They abruptly discussed what had happened with the monsters and made a decision to head on off the mountain toward home. Dr. George Moore and Dr. George Brooks never figured out what it was that they encountered, but they never forgot their harrowing experience at Gosainkund Pass during their return trip back down the Himalaya slopes from Tarke Ghyang 64 years ago—they were only able to theorize what it was. Dr. George Moore's memory of the incident was buried with him in the Christ Church Cemetery at Weems, Virginia in 2010. The Moore-Brooks sighting later attracted the attention of cryptozoologist Loren Coleman and he has expressed an opinion that the tailed, ape-like creature just might have been a Devil Monkey and that may be as good an explanation as any.

****

This brings to a close the Devil Monkey adventures which I have collected and placed into this book for the entertainment of my readers. One final warning which I often give is that if you would happen to encounter any kind of primate such as a baboon, monkey, gorilla, Bigfoot, or Devil Monkey—do not do anything to attract its attention. It is in your best interest to leave the area immediately and to notify the appropriate authorities. Do not trust any such animal, no matter how cute it may look. These creatures are wild animals and they are unpredictable. They are very strong and they can act in a very savage way. They have been known to attack and rip body parts from the victim's body. In some cases, they have been known to rip the victim's face off. You never know what an animal like that is capable of doing, especially if it feels that its territory is being threatened. As I always warn—never fall into the misguided belief that such a creature is your friend or trusted companion. You might be in for a surprise, which could lead to your demise.

THE END

OTHER BOOKS BY GEORGE DUDDING

61928437R00052

Made in the USA
Lexington, KY
26 March 2017